WARTIME INDUSTRY

Neil R. Storey

SHIRE PUBLICATIONS

Bloomsbury Publishing Plc

Kemp House, Chawley Park, Cumnor Hill, Oxford
OX2 9PH, UK

29 Earlsfort Terrace, Dublin 2, Ireland

1385 Broadway, 5th Floor, New York, NY 10018,
USA

E-mail: shire@bloomsbury.com

www.shirebooks.co.uk

SHIRE is a trademark of Osprey Publishing Ltd

First published in Great Britain in 2022

A catalogue record for this book is available from the
British Library.

ISBN: PB 978 1 78442 502 9
          eBook 978 1 78442 500 5
          ePDF 978 1 78442 501 2
          XML 978 1 78442 499 2

22 23 24 25 26   10 9 8 7 6 5 4 3 2 1

Typeset by PDQ Digital Media Solutions, Bungay, UK

Printed and bound in India by Replika Press Private Ltd.

Shire Publications supports the Woodland Trust, the
UK's leading woodland conservation charity.

COVER IMAGE

Front cover: Female workers at a Munitions factory in
the Second World War (Hulton-Deutsch Collection/
CORBIS/Corbis via Getty Images). Back cover image:
CC41 logo used on wartime 'utility' goods (see pages
50–51).

TITLE PAGE IMAGE

Exterior of the huge Ford Motor Company factory
by the Thames at Dagenham. Note the camouflage
applied to the chimneys and buildings, c.1943.

CONTENTS PAGE IMAGE

Bomber fuselages under repair at the LMS Railway
Carriage and Wagon Works at Derby, c.1942.

ACKNOWLEDGEMENTS

Images are acknowledged as follows:

© Hulton-Deutsch Collection/CORBIS/Corbis via
Getty Images, page 4; Imperial War Museums via
Getty Images, page 10; J. A. Hampton/Topical Press
Agency/Getty Images, page 16; Archives Branch,
Naval History and Heritage Command, Washington,
DC, page 33 (bottom); Gamma-Keystone via Getty
Images, page 12 (top); Harry Todd/Fox Photos/Getty
Images, page 59; Imperial War Museums via Getty
Images, page 21 (bottom); James Jarche/Popperfoto
via Getty Images, page 13 (top); Pat Keely/Imperial
War Museums via Getty Images, page 26; Popperfoto
via Getty Images/Getty Images, pages 14 (bottom),
and 58; SSPL/Getty Images, page 15; The National
Archives/SSPL/Getty Images, pages 17 (top), 36
(bottom).

All other images are from the author's collection.

CONTENTS

INTRODUCTION

This war is a war of machines. It will be won on the assembly line.

Time, 16 September 1940

The First World War had taken a horrific toll in lives lost by all sides. In 1918, Prime Minister David Lloyd George pledged that the efforts of the war years would now be applied to rebuilding Britain in peace time. Future Prime Minister Stanley Baldwin was to comment of some his fellow Conservative Party MPs in the 1918 Parliament, 'They are a lot of hard-faced men, who look as if they had done very well out of the war.' The government was now determined to stop lining the pockets of those who made munitions.

A 'Ten Year Rule' government guideline was adopted in 1919, stipulating that the armed forces were to plan their budgets based on the assumption that the British Empire would not be involved in a major war for the next decade. What funding was left for the military was pared back year on year under the 'Geddes Axe' – cuts by the Committee on National Expenditure chaired by Sir Eric Geddes.

For Britain, the cutbacks meant there would only be limited investment in its armed forces and weapons development. Consequently, its naval vessels, tanks, armoured fighting vehicles and aircraft were nowhere near as advanced or as plentiful as the stocks held by other nations, especially after the Nazis came to power in 1933,

OPPOSITE
Women workers at an iron and steel company at Park Gate, Rotherham, c.1940.

and started militarising Germany and rebuilding their stocks of armaments.

Despite the British government adopting a policy of appeasement, consideration had to be given to the state of Britain's navy, army and air force. The Defence Requirements sub-committee was formed in November 1933 to identify the most pressing deficiencies in Britain's armed forces and to suggest measures to redress them.

Concerns were raised in the British press over the expansion of Germany's air force, along with reports of secret weapons and the development of poison gas bombs and sprays that could be inflicted on civilian populations by enemy bombers. In reaction to this, the government announced that experts were being consulted on the best methods to combat gas attacks. The press was also informed in June 1934 that the Air Ministry had placed orders with barrage balloon manufacturers. Prime Minister Stanley Baldwin reiterated his old belief that if another war were to break out, no air force, however strong, could protect Britain's cities from being bombed. The press leapt on this statement, and columns of 'what if' scenarios, under headlines such as 'London's Real Peril' and 'London Helpless', appeared in national and local papers.

It was clear that the people of Britain not only needed reassurance that they would

Advert for Coventry Climax trailer pumps, which would be purchased by many factories for their works' volunteer fire fighters as part of their air raid precautions, 1939.

be protected in an aerial attack, but also more practical measures for the protection of the population. In July 1934, it was announced a scheme was being developed, and the Air Raid Precautions Department – based at the Institute of Mechanical Engineers in Princes Gate, London – was created the following year.

In October 1935, the Chemical Defence Research Department sent a memorandum to the Defence Requirements Committee, suggesting that somewhere in the region of 30 million respirators, commonly referred to as 'gas masks', would be required for the protection of Britain's civilian population. On 8 April 1936, Home Office Under Secretary Geoffrey Lloyd announced to Parliament that the government planned to accumulate stocks of respirators that would be issued free to the public in all areas exposed to the danger of air attack. It was to be a massive undertaking.

Rather than designing a civilian respirator from scratch, they used one that had been developed by Major John Ambrose Sadd, Superintendent of the Defensive Munitions Department at Porton, Wiltshire. In January 1935, he had patented a design for a simple respirator suitable for mass production for issue to civilians. The 'gas mask' consisted of a rubber face-piece held in place by three fabric straps, with celluloid windows for the eyes and a filter that could be attached to the mask by a thick band of rubber.

The government placed the contract for the manufacture of the face-pieces with established suppliers, such as the Avon Rubber Company at Melksham, Wiltshire, which was well known for its tyres, golf balls and sundries such as bath mats. There was also Henley Tyre and Rubber Co. of Gravesend, Kent, famous for its rubberised cables, tyres and tennis balls, and the Leyland & Birmingham Rubber Company, which had a particularly good reputation for rubber swimming hats and rubber flooring. All these companies had not only the expertise and equipment to make the masks, but also the

Training members of the public how to test if a gas mask is fitted properly, c.1938. If it is being worn correctly, the board will stick to the bottom of the filter when the wearer inhales.

research and development facilities to test and improve them if deficiencies were found.

New plants and dedicated facilities would, however, be required for the production of the thousands of filters that would need to be pressed out of metal and filled with an activated layer of charcoal and a particulate layer of Merino wool impregnated with Carbon Black. The Air Raid Precautions (ARP) Department contracted J.B. Baxter & Co. Ltd of Leyland with regard to the filling and assembly of the civilian respirators. Premises were obtained at the redundant Garden Street Mill, formerly one of the largest cotton manufacturing concerns in Blackburn. When the Government Respirator Factory was opened amid great publicity by Geoffrey Lloyd in January 1937, it employed a staff of three hundred – mostly young women – and it was reported that it would soon expand to over five hundred to produce 40 million gas masks at a rate of 500,000 a week. Once it had got into its stride of production, a time and motion study at the factory demonstrated that 30,000 respirators could be assembled by twenty-nine workers in eight hours.

Other factories, such as the diving equipment manufacturers Siebe Gorman and Avon, would take on the production of Civilian Duty Respirator and Service Respirator face-pieces and hose; the main supplier for Service Respirator containers was Barringer, Wallis & Manners Ltd of Mansfield, Nottinghamshire.

Between 1937 and the outbreak of war in September 1939, many other factories would be created and dedicated to the production of supplies under government contracts, such as stirrup pumps, trailer pumps, materials for air raid shelters, helmets for use on active service and the home front and other key equipment for ARP services. The Government Respirator Factory at Blackburn, however, will always have the distinction of being the first factory to be specifically created for the mass production of an item of equipment for the protection of the civilian population in the event of a war emergency. Tragically, the story does not end well. A short while after production began, the particulate layer of the gas mask filters was changed to Merino wool impregnated with asbestos. Many of those involved in the manufacture and filling of these filters were exposed to the asbestos particles and would suffer serious medical issues as a result in later life.

RAW MATERIALS AND SALVAGE

INDUSTRY RELIES ON fuel and raw materials, and in the Second World War the 'big five' that would be key to war production in all belligerent nations were coal, iron, steel, aluminium and timber.

In 1939 coal still powered many factories and engineering works. Some factories were running more electric machinery, but it was coal that fired the power plants that generated gas and electricity. It was the fuel for the majority of trains, and there were still plenty of steam-powered vessels at sea. At home, coal was the fuel that most people used in their open-hearth fires for heat. In the spring of 1940, the output of British coal mines was raised to nearly 5 million tons a week. The problem was that the labour force in the mines had declined through the hard times of the 1920s and '30s. Some pits had been forced to close. Although there were plenty of experienced miners who had been unemployed when war broke out, many jumped at the chance to 'do their bit' serving their country in full-time employment and joined up as soldiers. The younger men, aged eighteen to twenty-one, were in the first age groups to be conscripted for military service in 1939. Miners also took the opportunity to get out of the pits and earn better money in the ever-expanding munitions industry.

Those who were left working in the mines tended to be older men; some even returned to the pits after being retired for some years. They worked hard, but mining took its toll on the health of men who had worked for years at the coal face.

OPPOSITE
Peggy Barnett, a Land Army instructor, giving training in sawmill methods at the Women's Timber Corps Training Camp at Culford, Suffolk, c.1942.

Coal miners at work on a seam at a colliery in Britain during the 1930s.

One of numerous wartime adverts offering the public advice on how to make their domestic coal last longer, 1941.

GO EASY WITH THE POKER

Fires last longer when left alone. To be constantly poking the fire is wasteful.

The delivery of coal for household use is only part of a tremendous programme. Our whole War and Industrial Production depends on Coal, and its transport. But there are other products to be carried. Food, raw materials, munitions, the needs of the Fighting Services, all combine to make calls on Transport without precedent in our history.

That is why there is a shortage of coal in some areas. Everyone is anxious to help and you can do so by not being too particular about the kind of coal your merchant offers you and by making your coal and coke last as long as possible. For example :—

1. If you come in half-way through the evening, use gas or electric heating, to save lighting a fire.

2. Sift and use all cinders and use your heating and hot water sparingly.

Ask your supplier for free booklets on how to save coal and coke.

BE CAREFUL WITH **COAL** AND COKE

ISSUED BY THE MINES DEPARTMENT

Unable to work as hard as younger men, many continued to leave the industry. Output from the mines began to fall. The Ministry of Fuel was quick to act to control distribution and prioritise the allocation of coal. There were also high-profile campaigns across the media, instructing members of the public in fuel economy. A Fuel Efficiency Service was established under Dr E.S. Grummell in 1941, under which eighty-three full-time and 642 part-time voluntary fuel engineers visited nearly 24,000 factories over the later war years to help improve their fuel economy.

In 1942 the government assumed full operational control of the mines, and the Mines Department of the Board of Trade was made an independent ministry, with smart new headquarters and regional staff. The miners who remained down the pits worked long, hard shifts to help keep up production, and schemes were introduced for lads as young as fourteen to attend training pits to enable them to get to work down the mines. The problem was that there still were not enough miners to produce the supplies of coal needed to meet wartime demands. By October 1943, it was claimed Britain's coal reserves would last only three weeks.

To remedy the situation, Ernest Bevin, the Minister for Labour and National Service, devised a scheme whereby a ballot took place to allocate half the intake of conscripted men to serve down the mines rather than in the armed forces. A total of 48,000 'Bevin Boys' were conscripted, half by the ballot, with no other option, and the remainder came by choice in preference to serving in the armed forces. The first batch of 600 Bevin Boys began training for work in the pits on 18 January 1944. Their training lasted six weeks, four off site and two on. Between 1943 and 1945, one in ten conscripted soldiers was sent to work down the mines.

In wartime every armed force needed timber for a host of requirements, from wooden temporary buildings and barrack huts to wooden transport cases for munitions, food

A group of fourteen-year-old coal mining volunteers seated in a mine cage ready to descend to the training gallery at Ashington Colliery, May 1942.

FAR LEFT
Bevin Boys make the cover of *Boy's Own Paper*, November 1944.

LEFT
Members of the Women's Timber Corps carrying a pine tree trunk at a forest in Scotland, *c.*1942.

Making aluminium castings for a Merlin engine at a Rolls-Royce Factory, 1942.

and supplies. On the home front, temporary buildings provided homes for those who had been bombed out, and timber was used for the construction of factories, pit props for collieries, and telegraph poles. After imports were slashed due to the U-boat and mine menace at sea, home production of railway sleepers also had to increase from 800,000 to nearly 2 million that were required on main line railways every year.

More than 75 per cent of Britain's essential timber requirement was obtained by home timber production from the country's own forests and woodlands. During the course of the war, production of home timber rose from 450,000 tons to a peak of nearly 4 million tons a year. In considering this achievement, it should be remembered that members of the Women's Land Army (WLA) had worked in forestry since the beginning of the war, and the Women's Timber Corps (WTC) was created as a separate arm of the WLA in 1942. In due course WTC members, nicknamed 'Lumber Jills', took over just about every job in the industry.

Before the war, Britain had relied on imports for over half of the raw materials needed for the production of iron, steel and aluminium; so, with much of Europe and the Far East in the hands of

HOW YOUR SALVAGE HELPS TO MAKE A RESCUE LAUNCH

① SCRAP METAL
SCRAP IRON NEEDED FOR STEEL HULL. STEEL NEEDED FOR MAKING ENGINE AND MACHINE-GUNS. BRASS MAKES CARTRIDGE CASES. 3-PINT TIN KETTLE MAKES 40 MACHINE-GUN BULLETS. PHOSPHOR BRONZE NEEDED FOR PROPELLOR. COPPER FOR RADIO COMPONENTS

② ROPE, STRING, TWINE
MAKE NEW SHIP'S ROPE

③ WASTE PAPER
ONE ENVELOPE MAKES 50 WADS FOR MACHINE-GUN CARTRIDGES. TWELVE OLD LETTERS MAKE A CARTRIDGE BOX. WASTE PAPER ALSO MAKES GASKET WASHERS FOR ENGINE AND PROVIDES INSULATION FOR RADIO

④ SCRAP RUBBER
MAKES ELECTRICAL AND RADIO INSULATORS AND COMPONENTS

⑤ BONES
GIVE GLYCERINE—A COMPONENT IN CORDITE CHARGES FOR MACHINE-GUN CARTRIDGES

⑥ RAGS
COTTON RAGS MAKE SPECIAL GRADES OF PAPER FOR CHARTS ALSO ENGINE WIPERS

One of many posters created for salvage drives to show people how the items they were donating would help the war effort, c.1941.

OPPOSITE
Women steel workers shovelling slag from the furnace at a steel works in northern England, November 1943.

Axis occupation forces, by 1942 supplies dried up. The deficit would be made up by the first national recycling campaigns in the history of Britain. In the Second World War the term was 'salvage', and the British government was not going to leave anything to chance. Under Regulation 50 of the Defence

A National Salvage Campaign scrap iron dump donated by people of Malden and Coombe, Surrey, April 1940.

(General) Regulations, 1939, all manner of iron objects, such as garden railings, bedsteads and redundant agricultural machinery were removed and collected as voluntary donations at iron dumps set up around the country. Around 600,000 tons of iron was also salvaged from bombed areas as 'blitz scrap' to be melted down and recast. The scheme worked so well and so much scrap was collected that such an amount could never be processed by the munitions industry; after being stockpiled at corporation depot yards and on railway sidings, it was quietly sold off as scrap later in the war. There have even been claims that there was so much scrap iron it was taken out into the Thames estuary, where it was dumped by the barge load.

Either way, the by-product of taking railings by order and the collection of iron had been a highly successful propaganda exercise that evoked a 'we are all in this together' ethos at a time when cohesion and fortitude were very much needed for British morale. Subsequent wartime drives to collect scrap steel and aluminium also produced remarkable results that kept Britain's wartime industries supplied with these essential metals. Production of iron ore rose from a pre-war average of nearly 12.5 million tons a year to a wartime peak of 19.5 million tons. Aluminium also increased from 18,000 to 56,000 tons, achieving some of the biggest growths in home production during the war.

Salvage drives were tremendously successful. They were well organised by salvage leaders and teams, often from the

Women's Voluntary Service. Children were also encouraged to take part as Junior Salvage Stewards in organised collecting groups known as 'Cogs'. Each salvage drive was well publicised, with eye-catching posters festooning public buildings and advertising hoardings; there would be special films about the drive shown at local cinemas and adverts in magazines and newspapers. The uses to which each material being collected would be put was explained, such as bones that could be processed to make cordite, glue, soap or fertilizer; rubber that could be re-formed for military purposes, such as the linings of helmets; old clothes that could be turned into rags for engine wipers, camouflage netting or gun wadding; or paper that could be used in cartridge factories: as one poster pointed out, '20 periodicals make 1 seat for a pilot'. Money to pay for the war effort was also raised with national campaigns, such as The Spitfire Fund, Warship Weeks and War Weapons Week, to encourage people to buy War Savings and National Savings. The British public largely backed these drives, feeling that in doing so they were making a valuable contribution to the war effort.

One of the numerous eye-catching posters that were produced to motivate the public to buy War Savings during Warship Week, 1941.

Advert for Dagenham's War Weapons Week that was held 22–29 March 1941.

Now also built in the new world
BRITISH - DESIGNED MOSQUITOES
fly to the attack!

The de Havilland war effort is not confined to the British
Isles. An Empire chain of associated companies, forged
from 1927 onward, to-day forms a world dispersal system
of war production. Mosquitoes built in the Canadian
de Havilland plant now fly the Atlantic to augment the
output of British factories. When the war is won this great
British enterprise will be ready to serve the needs of peace.

DE HAVILLAND
AIRCRAFT · ENGINES · PROPELLERS

In the attack today – on the trade routes of the future

GREAT BRITAIN   AUSTRALIA   CANADA   INDIA   AFRICA   NEW ZEALAND

SHADOW FACTORIES

IN 1935, AFTER many years of military cutbacks, Britain's air force was only fifth among the air forces of the world. At the same time, in Germany, Hermann Göring was outlining his plans for the expansion of the German air force, blustering ideas of building aircraft factories capable of producing 2,500 aircraft a week. Prime Minister Stanley Baldwin announced there would be forty-one new squadrons for the RAF, but if the RAF were to be brought up to par, it would need at least 1,500 new aircraft too. The British aircraft industry had been reduced to a fraction of what it had been during the First World War. Despite there being established firms – such as Airspeed, Avro, Armstrong, Whitworth, Bristol, Fairey, Gloster, Hawker, Handley Page, Rolls-Royce, Short Brothers and Westland – none of them had the capacity to undertake mass production. They were capable of expansion, but this would take time, and to meet such demanding numbers of aircraft now being ordered they would need assistance.

To achieve this, a project was developed under Secretary of State Lord Swinton with Sir Herbert Austin, of the Austin Motor Company, whereby other engineering businesses with similar skill sets would take on aircraft production work in dedicated new premises known as 'Shadow Factories'.

The initial production work in March 1936, taken on by Austin Motors and Rootes Securities – best known for ownership of Hillman and Humber cars – was for the manufacture of airframes. Six weeks later, the aero engine

Machining a cylinder block for a Rolls-Royce aero engine, c.1942.

Shadow Scheme was launched, with Austin, Daimler, Rootes, Rover, Standard and Bristol Aeroplane Company working together in the No. 1 Engine Group, each taking on just one part of the manufacturing process of the Bristol Mercury aero engine.

The entire costs of the new Shadow Factories were borne by the Air Ministry, from the acquisition of land, factory construction and building services, plant and equipment, to all materials for manufacture and all labour costs, be they management, admin or production staff. The original plan stipulated that a reasonable number of aircraft components were to be produced by the factories; then, after the threat of war had died down (as it was anticipated it would at the time), the new works would be reduced to a maintenance cadre and the workers engaged in the parent works on the understanding they would be available to switch back over instantly at the approach of war conditions. In reality, the war demands just continued to grow and the workers never went over to their parent works.

It had originally been envisaged that the new factories would be erected near the extant main works of the motor car firms in the scheme – the idea being they would be both in the 'shadow' of the buildings and 'shadow' the technical know-how of their employees. Before the outbreak of war, they were not as secret as their name may imply. Reports of their progress appeared in national newspapers, and the factories received official visits from royalty, prominent politicians and dignitaries; even General Erhard Milch, the Chief Administrator of the Luftwaffe, and his entourage of senior officers, were given a tour of the Shadow Factories in Birmingham and Coventry during a week-long tour of RAF stations and establishments as guests of the Air Council in October 1937. Milch declared the Shadow Factories 'a great innovation' and was much impressed with the strides the aircraft industry had taken since his last visit eighteen months earlier.

Concurrent with the Shadow Scheme, Vickers (Aviation) Ltd, which had acquired the Supermarine Aviation Works in Southampton back in 1928, began production of airframes. English Electric also took on airframe and aircraft manufacture of Hampden and Halifax aircraft in conjunction with Handley Page. There were no teams at the Air Ministry designing aircraft; that was carried out by their manufacturers and the aeronautical engineers they employed, to requirements specified by the Air Ministry. If

the prototypes created by the companies fitted the bill, then a certain number would be ordered. Among the most notable of all the designers at the time was Sydney Camm at Hawker, best known for designing the Hawker Hurricane that went into production for the Air Ministry in 1936.

Cover of *Flight*, June 1938, introducing the Hawker Hurricane, designed by Sydney Camm.

There was also Reginald Joseph 'R.J.' Mitchell of Vickers Supermarine, who used the same technical skill he had developed over successive generations of Schneider Trophy seaplanes to design the Spitfire that first flew in prototype in March

Sir Frank Whittle, father of the jet engine, c.1942.

1936. Thank goodness Vickers Chairman Sir Robert McLean's oldest daughter Annie was a feisty young lady he called 'little spitfire' and he decided to name the aircraft after her; otherwise, the most iconic aircraft of the Second World War would have been known by Mitchell's preferred name of the 'Supermarine Shrew'.

The only significant aircraft design by a serving RAF officer was the turbojet engine pioneered by Frank Whittle in the 1930s. Allowed only to work a certain number of set hours outside his duties, Whittle received no Air Ministry support. Having only limited funds, he joined with two retired RAF servicemen to form Power Jets Ltd, and a prototype was created in 1937. Thankfully, contracts were placed to develop more, but financing the ground-breaking engine was always problematical, especially as it required over 8,000 modifications during its development. Despite a number of setbacks, Whittle never gave up, and in July 1944 the Gloster Meteor became the first and the only jet aircraft in the Allied forces to serve in combat during the war.

The initial Shadow Scheme was slow to progress, more through obstructive members of the senior management team than the scheme itself being faulty. When Sir Howard Kingsley Wood was appointed Secretary of State for Air in 1938, British factories were producing eighty war planes a month. The high-output engines required by the RAF were made by Armstrongs, Bristol, Napier and Rolls-Royce, who were all successfully employing a high number of efficient sub-contractors. In the spirit of 'many hands make light work', Wood tackled the issue by dropping the poor-performing contractors from aircraft production and repurposing their Shadow Factories to manufacture other essential wartime equipment. Others were placed under the management of an alternative company that had been running a successful Shadow Factory.

Two months before the outbreak of war in 1939 there were a total of thirty-one Shadow Factories either completed or under construction. The Air Ministry was responsible for 16 of these Shadow Factories: two were making aircraft carburettors; one made airscrews; another was producing bombs; and the remainder were producing airframes and aero engines. Under Kingsley Wood, production had risen to 546 warplanes a month by 1940, but the aircraft losses during the Battle of France and the Battle of Britain meant this was still not enough.

Winston Churchill was already aware of how acute the aircraft production situation had become when he took office as Prime Minister on 10 May 1940. Assertive action was required to increase aircraft production. Churchill had known the press baron Max Aitken, commonly known as Lord Beaverbrook, for many years. Beaverbrook had built up the *Daily Express* to be the largest national paper in the world, selling 2.25 million copies across the country every day. If he could achieve that, Churchill was confident Beaverbrook was the right man to entrust with such an important task; so, he appointed Beaverbrook as Minister of Aircraft Production on 14 May 1940.

Max Aitken, Lord Beaverbrook, Minister of Aircraft Production 1940–41.

Beaverbrook grasped the nettle and not only took over aircraft production but also controlled aircraft repairs and storage units. The Aeronautical Inspection Directorate – with its six divisions consisting of aircraft, armament, engines, aircraft equipment, materials and general stores, each with its own teams of experts with the relevant technical knowledge – was to be attached to or to tour works to quality check what was being produced by the factories and contractors. This was also brought under the aegis of the Ministry of Aircraft Production.

Beaverbrook developed works publicity and made radio and press appeals for more aircraft factory workers to join; candidates with some experience working in garages were particularly sought. All aircraft development work was postponed so full concentration could be given to immediate production for six months, and 'action squads' drawn from service officers were inaugurated to speed up the supply of general shop equipment and spare parts. The supervision of the Civilian Repair Organisation, which contracted the companies handling the repair of RAF aircraft and the reconditioning of parts salvaged from damaged aircraft, was also transferred to Beaverbrook's Ministry of Aircraft Production. A Director of Repairs and Maintenance was also appointed, who, with his

team, brought about greater co-operation between the parent companies and the firms dealing with their products.

Beaverbrook would brook no procrastination; production targets were raised by 15 per cent, and if companies underperformed they were removed and replaced. Beaverbrook would even take the initiative personally to ensure the required supplies were sent to the factories that needed them, even if it meant diverting them from their original intended destination. All this did not always make Beaverbrook a popular man with the Air Ministry, but he got the job done. Air Chief Marshal Hugh Dowding, the Head of Fighter Command during the Battle of Britain, paid tribute:

Women riveters and electricians working on the fuselage of a bomber at an aircraft factory, c.1942.

We had the organization, we had the men, we had the spirit which could bring us victory in the air but we had not the supply of machines necessary to withstand the drain of continuous battle. Lord Beaverbrook gave us those machines, and I do not believe that I exaggerate when I say that no other man in England could have done so.

The aircraft manufacturers continued to expand through the war. More Shadow Factories were created, and a huge array of sub-contractors were appointed; in fact, just about anywhere with workshops of a reasonable size capable of the work, from London Passenger Transport to the Derby Carriage and Wagon Works of the London Midland Scottish Railway, were turned over to war work. Aircraft manufacturers continued to meet new challenges throughout the war as aircraft were improved; new marks were introduced; and completely new aircraft developed. Particular pride could be shown in the Mosquito. So brilliant was its design and the efficiency of the factory concerned with its production that only 359 days elapsed between the arrival of the final drawings at the de Havilland Factory production office and the flight of the first Mosquito produced from its production line.

The growth of the aircraft industry during the war was truly remarkable, especially when it is considered that the work of the nineteen leading aircraft and aero engine companies was carried out at just fifty-two establishments at the beginning of 1938. By January 1943, there were over 473 establishments that employed 100 workers or more. The labour force of British aircraft firms had grown more than 4,000 per cent to a peak in 1944, when in excess of 1.8 million men and women were employed in aircraft manufacture.

OPPOSITE
Constructing a de Havilland Mosquito at the Hatfield factory, Hertfordshire, 1943. Note the distinctive wooden frames of the aircraft in the background.

Avro Lancaster bombers nearing completion at the A.V. Roe & Co. Ltd factory at Woodford, Cheshire, 1943.

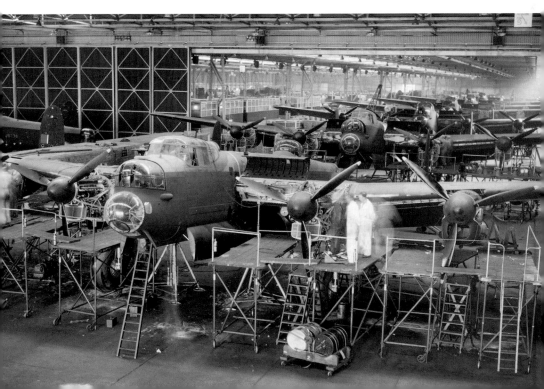

THE NAVY THANKS YOU

SHIPYARDS

T HE ANGLO-GERMAN NAVAL Agreement of 1935 had been intended to limit the German navy to a strength with which the Royal Navy could cope. The British assessment for the new standard of its naval strength, conducted in 1937, suggested that Britain could not afford a fleet capable of dealing with the German and Japanese navies.

It also raised questions as to whether the expenditure on rebuilding a Royal Navy battle fleet would be worthwhile if, as was feared at the time, the capital ships could easily be destroyed by aerial attacks. As a result, the lion's share of the British military spending budget was given over to the Air Ministry, and both the Admiralty and War Office would have to make do with what was left. Consequently, the 1938 Royal Navy ship building programme would consist of two 40,000-ton battleships, one aircraft carrier, seven cruisers, three submarines and three fast minelayers.

The best ships of the existing fleet were mostly of First World War vintage and were modernised through refits. It was hardly the shot in the arm the ship industry needed, and in the Northeast alone, even after war was declared in 1939, there were still 67,000 skilled shipyard workers who remained unemployed; many of them would soon take the opportunity to find employment by joining the armed forces. After the years of depression between the wars, by the time the shipbuilding industry was needed again its manpower was severely diminished. To ensure best use was made of

Launch of the cargo ship *Empire Voice* at the Clydeholm shipyard of Barclay, Curle & Co. Ltd, Glasgow, September 1940.

the remaining human and material resources, Britain's shipbuilding industry was brought under the control of the Admiralty and Sir James Lithgow, the Controller of Merchant Shipbuilding.

Rather than building mighty battleships, it was the smaller naval vessels – such as destroyers, sloops, corvettes and anti-submarine craft – that were in greatest demand. Many shipyards could take this sort of work on. One Royal Navy Volunteer Reserve officer would recall, when he was commissioning a new corvette in 1940, 'it seemed as if, up and down the Clyde, anyone who had ever handled a hammer had set up a pole in his back garden and started building a corvette.'

At the beginning of 1940, there were only 23,000 skilled workers available for mercantile ship production. Even though this increased to 35,000 by 1941, there was no time during the war that the shipyard labour force was equal to plant and berth capacity. The workforce left at the shipyards, after men of eighteen and up to their forties had been called up, was reduced to young lads, older men and those who had been judged medically unfit for military service. The older men were also at a disadvantage, because many had been out of shipyard work for such a long period that their physique had deteriorated and they were not up to the strenuous work.

As many women stepped into what had been male jobs, across trade and industry, just as they had done in the First World War, the managers and male workforces in shipyards seemed more misogynistic than ever and objected to the employment of women. When compared with all other industries, especially factories at that time, the number of women taken on by shipyards was relatively small. In the early years of the Second World War, at shipyards employing thousands, women would represent only about 10 per cent of the workforce. Janet Harvey's experience was typical of many women who entered the shipyards as a war worker. She had studied for three months to work as an electrician before joining Harland and Wolff's Fairfield shipyard in Govan in 1940 when she was eighteen. Decades later she recalled, 'It was horrendous. It was awful. All the men looking at us and whistling. It gradually quietened down and you got used to it but it wasn't the environment for young girls.'

Women were trained in a variety of light engineering trades at shipyards, such as welders, electricians' assistants, riveters, electric crane drivers, fitters, polishers, painters and joiners. They gained a reputation for being both conscientious and for doing a good job, which also led to resentment from some jealous male members of the workforce.

As the war progressed, more men were called for military service from shipyards. Women were also subject to conscription under the 1941 National Service Act, and with more women joining the available workforce, and the ever-pressing need for more ships,

Prime Minister Winston Churchill shaking the hand of sixteen-year-old George Smith, the youngest worker at Portsmouth dockyard, January 1941.

ABOVE LEFT
Electrically welding hatch bridle beams to a cargo vessel at a shipyard, c.1942.

ABOVE RIGHT
One of Britain's wartime women electric welders, c.1942.

the number of women employed in shipyards increased. They were also taken on at smaller boatyards around the country, working on smaller vessels, and their working experience here was often far better than in the bigger shipyards. In some boatyards there were even all-female working parties building smaller coastal craft.

When a fleet of invasion barges was needed for the Normandy landings, the craft were first built at shipyards. When the shipyards' space and time was prioritised for warships, however, the barge work was contracted to boatyards and even large commercial wood-working firms that had never built boats before. Hundreds of women were engaged in this work and the finishing of the landing craft, and on 6 June 1944 the boatyard and shop-fitter built barges all 'did their bit' transporting troops to the D-Day beaches.

Key to the consolidation of the successes achieved on D-Day and the support of Allied forces as they fought on into France – and arguably the greatest achievement of British

Civil Engineering during the war – was the construction of the Mulberry Harbours. The idea was a simple one: rather than attempting to seize an existing heavily defended harbour on the French coast, the British would create their own, in sections that could be assembled in the waters outside two of the D-Day beaches once they had been taken. The creation of the component parts of the harbours and their associated breakwaters was a massive undertaking.

Each completed Mulberry Harbour was designed to be approximately a mile in length and would stand about 30 feet above sea level at high tide. Each harbour would consist of 6 miles of flexible steel roadways that floated on steel or concrete pontoons, all of which would be protected by huge sunken caisson chambers that, when deployed, would fill with water to keep them on the seabed. The majority of the massive concrete caissons were built in hastily constructed dry docks on the rivers Thames and Clyde. Labour was enlisted from all manner of trades; at its peak some 45,000 personnel were employed on the project. The caissons and their components were towed across the Channel and were operational within

A newly completed LCT is commissioned, cheered on by women workers who helped to build it at formerly redundant shipyard, Alloa, Rosyth, April 1944.

twelve days of the initial landings; thousands of tons of hardware, weapons, equipment and supplies were soon rolling into Normandy.

All British shipyards did their bit in wartime, often working through the night under lighting, when air raids permitted, and carrying on through the daylight hours. Many workers would recall how they became oblivious to air raid sirens, claiming they were too busy concentrating on their work or didn't hear the siren, aircraft or even bombs exploding nearby over the noise of the work going on in the shipyard. The wartime production of both Merchant and Royal Navy ships was a remarkable achievement; for example, along the Clyde alone over 1.5 million tons of merchant shipping was built. Another remarkable record of production during the war years was achieved at Vickers Shipbuilding and Engineering Ltd at Barrow in Furness, which produced two aircraft carriers, two cruisers, an aircraft repair ship, twelve destroyers, thirty-five

"This remarkable achievement—by its very soundness of design alone—is consistent with that traditional high standard demanded for service in the Royal Navy."

A Motor Torpedo Boat—a notable contribution to the Defence of the Realm—like all the "S.P." range—a triumph of modern design and craftsmanship.

Designed by Hubert Scott-Paine. Constructed by
THE BRITISH POWER BOAT COMPANY, HYTHE, SOUTHAMPTON, ENGLAND

We Salute... and thank the magnificent men and women of all our fighting services — land, sea and air. Highly skilled and competent, they will demand of Peace exacting standards of specialisation. The Dunlop Rubber Company, so closely in touch with their needs in war, will be specially qualified to serve them in Peace.

DUNLOP "An army of Specialists"

Concrete Phoenix caissons, part of the Mulberry artificial harbour being constructed in Surrey Docks in Rotherhithe, April 1944.

transport vessels of various types and 112 submarines. At the height of construction flow during the war, a submarine was completed at the shipyard every two weeks.

One of the concrete Phoenix caissons afloat in its dock and ready for deployment to Normandy, painted by Dwight Shepler, 1944.

Victory Parade, Tunis, May 20th, 1943

Daimler
goes to war

THE DAIMLER COMPANY LIMITED · LONDON AND COVENTRY

MUNITIONS, TANKS AND MILITARY MOTORS

THE LARGEST MILITARY industries owned by the government during the Second World War were the Royal Ordnance Factories (ROFs) that produced munitions for Britain's fighting forces. During the war, High Explosive ROFs were created at Bridgwater, Drigg, Irvine and Pembrey, and there were Propellant ROFs manufacturing cordite at Bishopton, Ranskill, Sellafield and Wrexham. A number of Agency Factories, detached from the ROF organisation, were also built and owned by ICI Nobel.

There were also sixteen ROF filling factories that filled the various bombs, shells, grenades and cartridge cases manufactured by outside contractors. The largest of these was ROF Chorley (Filling Factory No. 1), built over a 928-acre site with extensive underground magazines. A number of the ROF filling factories were also managed as agency factories by private companies previously unconnected with the explosives industry, such as the famous corner house tea shop chain owner J. Lyons & Co., the Co-operative Wholesale Society (CWS), Courtaulds, Imperial Tobacco and Lever Brothers. To give some idea of the scale of production, between 1940 and 1945 nearly 52 million anti-aircraft shells, 90 million mortar bombs and in excess of 100 million grenades and mines were filled at the ROF filling factories. ROF factories also produced artillery, as did numerous private contractors. There was no holding back on the employment of women in any of these factories; one of the first ROF factories to turn out 1,000 guns

OPPOSITE
Wartime advert for the Daimler Motor Company, depicting some of its armoured cars on the parade held on 20 May 1943 to mark victory in the Tunisian Campaign.

Women workers checking 25-pounder artillery shells at the small arms factory of J & F Pool Ltd, Hayle, Cornwall, 1943.

a month had a sizeable workforce, three-quarters of whom were women. There was also a massive army central ordnance depot for vehicles, spare parts and accessories at the former National Shell Filling Factory at Chilwell in Nottinghamshire.

The government also owned the Royal Small Arms Factory at Enfield, where service revolvers (also produced by Webley & Scott of Birmingham), the many variants of the .303 Lee Enfield rifle and the Bren Light Machine gun (a superbly accurate piece, designed at the Czech Zbrojovka Brno Factory ['Br'] and produced under licence by Enfield ['en'], hence the name 'Bren') were manufactured. The Enfield factory also had two dispersal factories, ROF Fazakerley in Liverpool and ROF Maltby, South Yorkshire, producing rifles and machine guns.

The Sten gun, first issued in 1941, was also developed at Enfield. Like the Bren, this weapon reflects the names of its developers, Major Reginald Shepherd ('S'), Harold Turpin ('t')

and Enfield ('en'). Consisting of a total of just 51 parts, Stens and their parts were produced under contract by a huge number of companies, large and small. The wooden furniture and some of the features of the Mark I Sten that were considered superfluous were removed in the next version. Consequently, the average cost of the composite parts of a Sten was

reduced to approximately 15 shillings. The Mark II Sten became the standard service sub-machine gun of British and Commonwealth forces, and through its various Marks some 3 million Sten guns were produced during the war.

Mrs D. Cheatle from Sheffield operating a capstan lathe at a munitions factory in Yorkshire, 1942.

The .303 Lee Enfield rifles carried by most of the British Army were only produced by Birmingham Small Arms (BSA) at Small Heath in 1939. After the city suffered severe damage over three air raids in 1940, production was dispersed over Shadow Factories mostly in the West Midlands and Worcestershire, where BSA continued to produce rifles, machine guns, 2-pounder gun carriages, Hispano cannon, Oerlikon 20mm cannon, Boys anti-tank rifles and rockets, as well as its excellent motorcycles and bicycles. At its peak BSA was operating out of sixty-seven factories, and numerous companies were making their products under licence.

Small Arms Ammunition (SAA) was produced at four factories in 1939. The high demand in wartime saw a total of twenty new factories engaged in the production of components or the filling and assembly of rounds. At the height of production during the war, there were also over 1,500 firms, strategically distributed all over Britain, engaged in some capacity in the production of ammunition. Well over 100,000 operatives were employed in small arms factories, 70,000 of whom were women. These factories would supply over 12 million rounds of all calibres to the fighting forces during the war.

OPPOSITE
Women working on 6-pounder artillery gun barrels at a Royal Ordnance Factory, c.1941.

Building Bren gun carriers at the Ford factory at Dagenham in Essex, c.1943.

Wilkinson Sword at Acton had been one of the leading contractors, and had produced bayonets and swords for the British Army since the nineteenth century. The firm was awarded the contract to produce the first 1,500 Fairbairn Sykes 'FS' fighting knives for commandos in 1940. These superbly designed and manufactured knives were ordered under a deliberately vague description as 'hunting knives' to obfuscate their true purpose. Sheffield, the home of British steel, played its part too, with the likes of John Clarke & Son joining in production of the Second Pattern of the 'FS' fighting knives. Sanderson Bros, renowned for their saw blades, made a remarkable contribution to the war effort too, producing paravane plane units for minesweepers, parts for torpedoes, hard-wearing clutch plates for armoured fighting vehicles, supplying steel for tools, gun and rifle parts, and producing over 1 million bulletproof plates.

The new generation of Lee Enfield rifles also required a new bayonet. The first 75,000 No. 4 Mark I bayonets with distinctive cruciform blades were produced by the sewing machine manufacturer Singer at their Clydebank factory between 1941 and 1942. A simplified Mark II 'pig sticker' bayonet without the cruciform milling was produced by Singer and other companies in Britain, Canada and America; over 3 million of these were produced over the years 1942–44. A further modification saw the Mark II* produced by a number of companies in the UK, primarily the power loom manufacturers Howard & Bullough of Accrington, Prince-Smith & Stells of Keighley, Lewisham Engineering and Baird Manufacturing Company of Belfast. The No. 36 Mills fragmentation grenade was purchased in huge numbers from its developers, the Mills Munitions Factory in Birmingham, which used contractors to create the parts, such as grenade bodies and base plugs. The No. 69 grenade, made entirely out of Bakelite, was mass produced by De La Rue Plastics Ltd, a subsidiary of Thomas De La Rue and Co., the banknote printers. All of these grenade bodies were then sent to the ROFs to be filled with ammonal or amatol explosives.

The Mills Equipment Company of Victoria Street, London, had made their name with the manufacture of the 1908 Pattern 'Webbing' Equipment during the First World War, and they

BELOW LEFT
Women workers at the Royal Ordnance Factory at Fazakerley, Liverpool, working on Sten gun breech block parts, 1943.

BELOW RIGHT
Women workers finishing the assembly of Sten guns, c.1943.

A heavy-duty power saw operator with brightly coloured bars of steel in the background, c.1942.

would be at full production again, and using no fewer than an additional thirty-one different companies during the Second World War. From 1939, Mills was operating in the true spirit of 'The Group System', where any company that was capable of producing a product to standard and delivered on time could be a manufacturer – from Bagcraft Limited, Barrow Hepburn and Gale Ltd, County Screen Company and Crown Bedding, to May Harris Gowns, Princess Silk Shade, Rover Cars and The Teddy Toy Company. Whether they produced pistol holsters, ammunition pouches, entrenching tool holders, map cases, small or large packs, they all made parts of the new 1937 Pattern Equipment.

If Britain was going to have a modern, mechanised army, then mass production of tanks needed to be addressed too. The facilities offered by railways such as the LMS at Derby, in its day the largest carriage and wagon works in Europe, and the skilled hands of railway engineers, were ideal for tank construction. Railway locomotive builders suspended work on new builds and the massive carriage and wagon sheds of railway companies, while keeping their locos and rolling stock well maintained, stopped their carriage building and began to work on government orders, from simple machinery and casting jobs up to the complete assembly of tanks and aircraft.

Thanks to motor cars becoming affordable in the 1920s and '30s, more people had become car owners than ever before. With the development of a range of road transport vehicles and delivery vans, rather than dwindling over the inter-war years, the British motor industry and allied trades had grown apace and by 1939 were employing over a million people.

Motor factories had been quick off the mark to prepare for war. The blackout of their many windows was often achieved far more rapidly than that of other factories, because they set their spray painters to the task, applying a coating of opaque paint to every pane. On 4 September 1939, however, some motor factory workers had no work in front of them, as new production was halted and they were transferred, for the time being, to help get the later stages of production on the last of the pre-war vehicles completed. Orders for war-related work soon arrived; typical of these was an order for five hundred cars of over 16hp to have the rear half removed and replaced by an ambulance body.

Manufacturing firms, many of which had never worked on munitions before, had to adapt quickly to take on this new work. In motor factories, machines that had made stub axles had to turn out horns for sea mines; machines making gear blanks were adapted to make depth-charge pistols for anti-submarine work. Others, making brake drums, had to be retooled to make star shells to illuminate enemy surface craft. As had been the case with some aero engines, military authorities or the original design companies would often

Assembly floor at a factory producing Crusader tanks, 'somewhere in England', 1941.

not allow complete engines, items of technical equipment or weapons to be made in any single factory outside their own, especially if it was a new development and needed to remain secret. Many of those who were making such items did not know what it was for with any certainty until after the war. Arthur Askey caught the mood perfectly in his popular monologue 'The Thing-Ummy-Bob', in which he sings about his lady friend who works on munitions:

> It's a ticklish sort of job making a thing for a thing-ummy-bob
> Especially when you don't know what it's for
> But it's the girl that makes the thing that drills the hole that holds the spring that works the thing-ummy-bob that makes the engines roar.
> And it's the girl that makes the thing that holds the oil that oils the ring that works the thing-ummy-bob that's going to win the war.

Covenanter tanks designed by the LMS Railway Company and in service with 9th Armoured Division entraining at Blaydon, Newcastle, October 1941.

During the Second World War, the designs for new tanks came increasingly from the railway engineers and motor companies producing them, such as Vickers, Vauxhall, Nuffield, Leyland and Rolls-Royce. As tank production increased, even more contractors with suitable works were brought in to increase production. In turn, a number of these works produced a variety of tanks, and armoured fighting vehicles; they even turned their hands to Horsa and Hamilcar gliders.

Between July 1939 and May 1945, British industry produced 27,528 tanks and self-propelled guns, 26,191

armoured cars and 69,071 armoured personnel carriers. On the LMS alone, they made Cruisers, Covenanters, Matildas and Centaur tanks along with thousands of spare parts. The LMS workshops worked day and night, producing 70,000 steel castings, and thirty-four drop hammers worked continuously to turn out 4 million stampings for war equipment, ranging from planes and tanks to armoured fighting vehicles and gun shells. Birmingham Railway Carriage & Wagon Co. produced Churchill, Valentine, Cromwell and Challenger tanks and even produced original prototype tanks.

Vauxhall Motors was outstanding in producing Churchill tanks from its Luton works. It also employed 12,000 people on lorry production lines, who were making nearly a thousand finished vehicles every week. Between September 1939 and

Factory workers on a lunch break beside the Matilda II tank they are constructing, 1942.

Advertisement from 1945, proudly showing the various tanks made during the war by the Birmingham Railway Carriage & Wagon Co. Ltd.

Thanks for the Guns!

Guns are still a vital need, and the Motor Industry will continue to make them until the day of Victory. Then, the Industry will whole-heartedly support the Government with well-founded plans for full employment.

THE MOTOR INDUSTRY

MANUFACTURE · DISTRIBUTION · MAINTENANCE

Production for Victory

A thanks to the British Motor Industry widely published in the later war years.

BSA Motorcycles advert looking forward to peacetime in 1945.

VE Day 1945, Vauxhall supplied no fewer than 209,096 Bedford lorries to the armed forces. Let us not forget the fastest men on the ground, the Despatch Riders, who had to depend on reliable motorcycles to do their job. Out of the 400,000 motorcycles made by British motorcycle manufacturers, 115,000 were produced by BSA.

The ethos was 'get the job done', and it is embodied in the story related by Charles Graves in *Drive for Freedom* (1945), of one motor factory suddenly ordered to increase its production of iron castings from 40 to 140 tons per week. To achieve this, a new foundry had to be built, but with castings being so acutely short at the time, it was to be achieved without loss of production. This meant that the new building had to be erected over the top of the old one, and six different levels of floor made into one level without any delay in output.

Factories involved in government work were often instructed to camouflage their buildings and chimneys. Camouflage officers, many of them with a background in film and theatre set creation, would advise the best methods and suitable paint schemes. To many on the ground, the strange patterns and shades of paint were the subject of derision; from the air, where such a subterfuge really mattered, it was quite often effective. The factories seldom disappeared completely after being camouflaged but at least they no longer stood out.

After the creation of the Local Defence Volunteers in May 1940 and especially after Churchill took an interest in the organisation and retitled them Home Guard,

CIVVY STREET SILHOUETTE

Five years of war service have proved, what every pre-war motor-cyclist knew, the value of B.S.A. Reliability.

Out of 400,000 Motor Cycles supplied to British Forces by the British Motor Cycle Industry, 115,000 were produced by B.S.A.

B.S.A., leaders of the Motor Cycle Industry, will give you even better service in the days to come.

BSA MOTOR CYCLES

WAR WHEELS YESTERDAY – YOUR WHEELS TOMORROW

B.S.A. Cycles Ltd., Birmingham, 11

factories were expected to raise their own units. These units would be part of their county Home Guard organisation but would have a specific remit to defend their factories. They would usually wear the same uniforms as the other local units, but some, such as Vickers Armstrong, would have cap badges that were unique in design. Others, such as Morris Motors and Swallow Sidecars, would have the standard issue cap badges of their parent county regiment but made unique by the addition of distinguishing letters.

By 1941 things were still tough going as British manufacturers strove to meet the supplies demanded by wartime. Imported goods and raw materials had been slashed, and to make matters worse, America had maintained neutrality since the outbreak of war and would not supply munitions to the belligerent nations. Britain had received a great deal of sympathy from the American public after the Fall of France, and finally President Roosevelt tabled a Lend-Lease Bill, by which means America would supply 'any defence article' to any country whose defence the President deemed vital to the protection of the United States. The Bill was passed, and America could supply arms to Britain. After the Japanese attack on Pearl Harbor, America joined the Allies, the Anglo-American Mutual Aid Agreement was signed in 1942, and billions of pounds worth of weaponry, tanks, military vehicles and uniforms were supplied by the crate load to Britain. The country also received over £3.5 billion in weaponry, uniforms and equipment from Canada. But British industries were still very much needed to do their bit for war production.

'Purely from a publicity point of view, the necessity for camouflage suits us very well.' With so many factories camouflaged, *Punch* injects some humour to the situation in October 1943.

BATTLE DRESS, BOOTS AND UTILITY GOODS

A S THE STORM clouds of the Second World War gathered in 1939, the British government was determined there would not be the same shortages of material for British Army uniforms that had been experienced back in 1914. The Ministry of Supply established the Wool Control with the legal power to direct production of the country's yarns and fabrics. The Wool Control became the sole importer and supplier of wool in Britain, and a strict system of rationing supplies was introduced whereby, initially, uniforms and garments for the armed forces were given priority, export trade second, and home production for civilians would be third. To ensure there was an adequate supply of wool, the British government purchased the entire wool clips of Australia, New Zealand and South Africa each year up to 1945. To give an idea of the scale of the deal, the purchase price of the clips from the three countries for the 1943–44 season exceeded 100 million pounds. The Ministry of Supply also created the Cotton Control, with responsibility for the supplies of raw material and for planning production up to the loom state cloth (the untreated woven cloth direct from the loom). Over a third of production was allocated for military use – some 300 million pounds in weight of yarn and 600 million yards of woven fabric every year.

From the outbreak of war, the Ministry of Supply switched the major British civilian clothing and footwear manufacturers to government contracts, making uniforms, equipment and

OPPOSITE
Wartime advertisement for Sylko cottons – shortages meant it was more important than ever to repair, repurpose and even make one's own clothes.

A 1941 advertisement for 'Viyella' regulation colour service shirts, only available for officers to purchase from high-class hosiers and outfitters.

military footwear. The factories of Montague Burton, one of the country's largest high street gentleman's outfitters, made a quarter of all British uniforms during the war. Burton was in a very good position to undertake this work, with his fourteen factories and flagship works at Burmantofts in Leeds that employed 1,000 men and 9,000 women, producing 30,000 suits a week. The Fifty Shilling Tailors made uniforms too, as did independent factories such as F.W. Harmer of Norwich, J. Compton, Son & Webb, Town Tailors Ltd, Denhams (1933) Ltd, Harry Levine Ltd of London, William Templeton & Sons, J & J Mendes Ltd, Bairstow, Sons & Co. Ltd, M. Belmont & Co. and even the Dunlop Rubber Co. Ltd, to name but a few. Most of these factories were producing wool serge battledress jackets and trousers – the durable, disposable and interchangeable standard kit for the fighting forces – but they could equally adapt to produce khaki drill, jungle greens, flying suits or Denison smocks. The army alone was supplied with the following quantities of battledress (trousers and jackets): 1940, 17.5 million; 1941, nearly 17 million; 1942, 9.5 million; and over 10 million in 1943. The dip in quantities supplied to the army in 1942 was because production at some of the companies was switched in late 1941 to the production of dark blue battledress uniforms for the Civil Defence, and air force blue battledress for RAF aircrew and Royal Observer Corps.

For Service of every kind

For the man of war and man-at-ease – a Viyella Service shirt. He will appreciate its orthodox yet comfortable tailoring, its capacity for remaining always the same after repeated wash and wear.

In regulation Khaki, White and Air Force Blue (Authorised colour 'Viyella' No. 31870), 17/9 (with two collars, 22/4). 'Viyella' Service Socks in Khaki and Black, 4/1. 'Viyella' Ties in Khaki and Black, 3/-.

OBTAINABLE FROM HIGH-CLASS HOSIERS AND OUTFITTERS   WRITE FOR THE NAME OF YOUR NEAREST SUPPLIER TO
WM. HOLLINS & CO. LTD., VIYELLA HOUSE, NOTTINGHAM. OVERSEAS REPRESENTATIVES AND AGENTS THROUGHOUT THE WORLD

'Viyella' SERVICE SHIRTS

Leather Control was established for British manufacture, but much of the leather used for civilian shoes was unsuitable for service footwear, especially the army's ammunition boots, which required both heavy sole leather and thick leather uppers. Home-grown British leather could provide about 25 per cent of the leather needed, and the balance had been imported from South America. Fortunately, Germany had withdrawn as a buyer there, and Britain was able to purchase sufficient quantities until 1941, when the U-boat menace

Manufacturing footwear for the Women's Royal Naval Service at a Midlands factory, 1944.

Good, stout military service style boots from Saxone, October 1940.

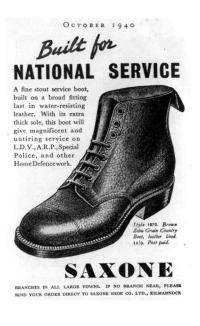

OCTOBER 1940

Built for

NATIONAL SERVICE

A fine stout service boot, built on a broad fitting last in water-resisting leather. With its extra thick sole, this boot will give magnificent and untiring service on L.D.V., A.R.P., Special Police, and other Home Defence work.

Style 1870. Brown Zebu Grain Country Boot, leather lined. 32/9. Post paid.

SAXONE

BRANCHES IN ALL LARGE TOWNS. IF NO BRANCH NEAR, PLEASE SEND YOUR ORDER DIRECT TO SAXONE SHOE CO. LTD., KILMARNOCK

sank a number of supply vessels carrying the hides and imports were slashed; supplies remained strained for the rest of the war. Britain was, at least in those days, a great country for mending things, and a huge rolling programme for the repair and rebuilding of damaged and worn army boots was developed to bridge the gap in service boot supplies.

Across all military services there were over sixty-five different types of footwear, from fleece-lined flying boots for aircrew and high-leg despatch rider boots to plimsolls used when service personnel engaged in physical training. In every instance, if leather was required, great lengths were taken to prevent waste, and if a sole could be replaced with one of another material, such as rubber or the thinner leather soles used on shoes, this was done.

Clothes rationing was introduced on 1 June 1941 and the Utility Scheme was launched soon after, with the aim of creating clothing and shoes from government-controlled materials that would guarantee quality and value for money. Precious coupons expended would cover a huge range of goods, from clothes and fabric products to furniture. Every garment or product made under the scheme was to bear an eye-catching mark to show it complied with the scheme, and the Board of Trade held a competition among design companies to create it. It was won by Reginald Shipp of Hargreaves, who based his design on the letters and number CC41 (Civilian Clothing 1941). It became known simply as 'The Cheeses', because the stylised circle letter Cs looked like round cheeses with a wedge cut out.

Less than a year later, clothing and shoe manufacturers were subject to The Making of Civilian Clothing (Restrictions) Order passed in March 1942. This limited the amount of cloth that could be used in the manufacture of each garment, with the idea of saving labour and reducing manufacturing costs. Battledress uniforms were already being made to a simpler pattern, with pleats removed from breast pockets, lining reduced, and, as brass became scarce, even the brass 'dish' buttons were replaced with plastic ones. Now the same economies would be extended to civilian clothes. For women,

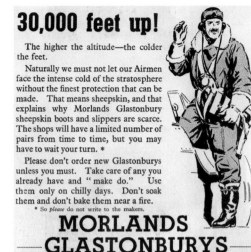

30,000 feet up!

The higher the altitude—the colder the feet.

Naturally we must not let our Airmen face the intense cold of the stratosphere without the finest protection that can be made. That means sheepskin, and that explains why Morlands Glastonbury sheepskin boots and slippers are scarce. The shops will have a limited number of pairs from time to time, but you may have to wait your turn. *

Please don't order new Glastonburys unless you must. Take care of any you already have and "make do." Use them only on chilly days. Don't soak them and don't bake them near a fire.

* So *please* do not write to the makers.

MORLANDS GLASTONBURYS

A sheepskin slipper with soft leather sole and a cosy turnover top.

A wartime ladies' ankle boot—sheepskin lined. Warm, serviceable, and neat.

Morlands Glastonburys – an enormously popular boot for quick donning, and the warmth they offered if one had to dash down the shelter at night.

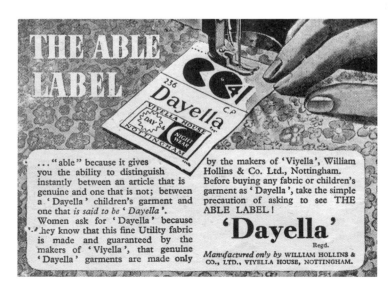

THE ABLE LABEL

... "able" because it gives you the ability to distinguish instantly between an article that is genuine and one that is not; between a 'Dayella' children's garment and one that *is said to be* 'Dayella'. Women ask for 'Dayella' because they know that this fine Utility fabric is made and guaranteed by the makers of 'Viyella', that genuine 'Dayella' garments are made only by the makers of 'Viyella', William Hollins & Co. Ltd., Nottingham. Before buying any fabric or children's garment as 'Dayella', take the simple precaution of asking to see THE ABLE LABEL!

'Dayella'

Regd.

Manufactured only by WILLIAM HOLLINS & CO., LTD., VIYELLA HOUSE, NOTTINGHAM.

'Dayella' fabrics were proud to display the 'CC41' utility cloth and clothing label.

the number of buttons and seams on their garments would be limited, and pleats, ruching, embroidery, braid and lace were all banned in the production of dresses and blouses. Skirts were limited to three buttons, six seams, two box pleats and only one pocket. The width of belts, collars and sleeves was also heavily restricted, and a maximum of four buttons was permitted on a coat. No shoes could have open toes or heels higher than 2 inches.

Men's suits could only be single breasted, and buttons on cuffs, flaps over pockets, turn ups, zips, elastic in waistbands and double shirt cuffs were all banned; even the standard length of shirts was shortened. Belts on coats and leather or metal buttons were also not allowed. Jackets were to be cut shorter, pleated jacket backs were forbidden, and trouser legs could be no more than 19 inches in circumference. Pyjama pockets and tailcoats were no longer permitted because they were

not considered essential or useful. Even manufactured socks were not to exceed 9½ inches in height.

In 1942, the Board of Trade commissioned a team from the Incorporated Society of London Fashion Designers, including Norman Hartnell, Hardy Amies and Bianca Mosca, to create a range of 'utility clothing'. The result was thirty-two designs produced from four basic outlines. It was hoped the use of top designers would ensure that utility clothes were not seen as the 'uniform' that some feared. It was also stipulated that manufacturers were to make their utility clothing as vibrant as possible. Eventually, two-thirds of material available for civilian clothing during wartime went into the manufacture of utility clothes. The Board of Trade was acutely aware that the scheme would succeed only if people believed they would not end up in unattractive clothes or some sort of state uniform.

The joyous range of the bold colours of Moygashel utility rayon fabrics, 1943.

Many people were glad that government controls were being placed on the quality, prices and availability of goods. The robust quality of the garments was certainly a selling point, but the term 'utility' carried a stigma of utilitarian style with it, and people would complain, as people often do, that the products were 'never as good as what we had before the war'.

THE WORKFORCE

THE YEARS BETWEEN the wars, during which so many had been unemployed, meant there was a ready and willing workforce when war broke out in 1939. However, as we have seen, many of these men volunteered or were conscripted into the armed forces. There were plenty of women to take their place, but some industries were still not welcoming them. In an effort both to maximise the workforce and give employers no more room for excuses, it was made compulsory for women aged nineteen to forty-five, subsequently increased to fifty (the only exceptions being mothers with children under fourteen living with them), to register at employment exchanges from March 1941.

The National Service (No. 2) Act of December 1941 brought about conscription for women for the very first time in British history. Initially, the women eligible for call-up were those who were unmarried and aged between twenty and thirty. Later this was extended to married women in the same age group. They were urged to join the women's branches of the military services, but those not wishing to do so could opt to do their national service in factories or in home front services such as Civil Defence or the Women's Land Army. By 1943, approximately 90 per cent of single women and 80 per cent of married women in Britain were involved in war work.

There were also a number of schemes whereby mothers with young children or care commitments could work part time. Initially, older female neighbours were encouraged

OPPOSITE
Colonel W.M. Tickler (of the famous jam making family) and some of the 250 working men of the Maidenhead 'Lunch Hour Brigade', who volunteered to spend their lunch hours in military training, June 1940.

Women war
workers sewing
cartridges in the
Cordite Section
of ROF Bridgend,
January 1942.

by posters and adverts stating 'Caring for war workers' children is a National Service' to act as 'nurseries' for the young children of neighbours so they could go to work. As demands for war production grew, a new government scheme created day nurseries for workers' children in industrial cities and towns across the country. Some women even had their children fostered and went away to work full time at one of the munitions factories. Newspapers regularly published the notable stories of the workers' efforts. Typical was one that appeared in local and national newspapers in February 1941, when it was announced some 2,666 Tyneside women had already left their homes for munitions work; this article was accompanied by an appeal for thousands more to come and join them.

The report also highlighted that the starting wage for women aged eighteen and over for a forty-seven-hour week varied from 31s to 38s. Free fare and reimbursement for travel were given for the initial journey; the factory work was described as needing only a minimum of training and offered the reassurance, 'most women could pick it up within the first fortnight of employment'. The actual earnings for those at the new factories averaged 40s–45s a week. When staff became more experienced, they could earn up to 60s a week, and when fully skilled a pay packet of 75s plus overtime awaited them. It was not a bad wage at all, and for many women it was a chance to escape the ties of home and actually earn their own money or a decent wage for the first time. There were also many opportunities for women and men unable to join the military services to work on the supply lines of industry, on railways, canals, docks, for the post office and as lorry drivers.

Any workers who were not supplied with working overalls by their employers faced a problem after clothes rationing was introduced. Schemes such as 'Mrs Sew and Sew' and 'Make Do and Mend' were introduced to help people mend and renew their old clothes, but working clothes wore out and it became hard to replace them under the original coupon scheme. A solution was offered in September 1942, when it was announced workers were to receive ten extra clothing coupons during the current rationing period – a scheme called the 'Industrial Ten'. Newspapers and government information sheets made clear that every man and woman who came within the category usually called 'manual workers' would be covered by the scheme, including farm labourers, miners and steel workers. The coupons would entitle the bearer to purchase either three utility overalls, two and a half boiler suits, two and a half pairs of industrial safety boots, two cotton shirts or more than one pair of boots. Applications for the coupons had to be made through the worker's trade union

'Women of Britain Come into the Factories' poster, first published in 1941. Philip Zec's striking artwork has made this one of the most iconic poster images of the Second World War.

WOMEN · OF · BRITAIN
**COME INTO
THE FACTORIES**
ASK AT ANY EMPLOYMENT EXCHANGE FOR ADVICE AND FULL DETAILS

or employer. It was intended that any deficits in the supplied coupons would be made up from the worker's own clothing allowance, but many joked about what they would do with half of a pair of working boots.

Day-to-day working was often interrupted by air raid alerts in many areas of the country. This did not always mean an enemy aircraft had passed over or the area was bombed, but people would take shelter if they heard the siren sound. Alerts without actual enemy action were frequent, and hundreds of precious working hours were being lost. So, in many areas where this was happening, a second siren or 'crash warning' system was created. Spotters, usually working in pairs, would be positioned on the roof, on a suitable high spot nearby or even on a specially constructed tower to keep watch. If an

Women factory workers machine-stitching parachute canopies. Each colour represented the type of supply being dropped, May 1944.

A roof spotter at the London, Midland & Scottish Railway ready to sound the 'crash warning' if an enemy aircraft approached, November 1940.

enemy aircraft was seen heading directly for their factory, they would then sound the 'crash warning', coloured lights would often be turned on to alert employees inside noisy factories, and the workforce would then take shelter.

Air raids took place throughout most of the war. It is often forgotten that between 1941 and 1944, when the focus of air raids was no longer on London, towns, cities and ports across Britain were targeted and subjected to 'tip and run' raids by enemy bombers. As a result, there were many workers who would turn up at their place of employment the morning after a raid to discover it had been badly damaged or even completely burnt out. Businesses were pretty good at bouncing back in wartime. If it was a matter of clearing up, everyone would lend a hand, or if the damage had been severe, the factory would often soon be up and running again in prefabricated buildings. Some manufacturers, especially those on government contracts, even dispersed their works to premises outside the towns and cities of their original factories before they themselves were damaged.

If employers were successfully to maintain productivity, it was essential to keep up morale. Canteens had to be provided by law for any factory with more than one hundred employees. Radio programmes, such as 'Workers Playtime', were often played through workplaces or piped into canteens on loud speakers, ENSA concert parties would come and perform, and film and radio personalities of the day would pay morale-boosting visits. Gracie Fields was one of the most popular singers and entertainers of the war years; her pre-war song 'Sing as We Go' was revived as the anthem for working people on the home front. Born in Rochdale, 'Our Gracie', as she was affectionately known, visited industrial areas all over the country, especially the North, to sing live in concert to huge audiences of factory and shipyard workers.

If one person epitomised the women workers of the time, it was twenty-six-year-old 'Nan' Jackson, who worked in a paint store at a Scottish shipyard. Her work consisted of lifting one-hundredweight drums of paint on and off delivery lorries. For a six-hundredweight cask, she would ask for help from the foreman, but she would regularly carry two hundredweight bags of shellac on her back. In her forty-five-minute dinner break, Nan would rush home to make a meal for her elderly

The Fire Patrol at Frank Price (Norwich) Ltd, c.1941.

father and her sister's children. Nan's sister had sadly died earlier in the war, and she had taken over the care and the expense of five children, the eldest of whom was twelve and the youngest four. Monday night Nan called 'steamy night', when she did the family laundry in the wash house and would get to bed about 1.00 a.m. In between times, she washed fourteen pairs of white socks 'to keep them going'. Nan, and many others like her, would also take turns as firewatchers; others would be part-time Civil Defence workers and members of other wartime organisations. When women like Nan and war workers in general were asked in their later years how they found the energy and drive to juggle so many responsibilities, the reply would often be given with a shrug, and they would say quite casually, 'We just got on with it.'

With the end of the war in 1945, the armed forces began the process of demobilising over 4 million male and female service personnel. Hopes for a new future had seen the Labour Party win a landslide victory in the 1945 general election. The aim was for full employment. More affordable housing, as well as council houses, was built than ever before; town and country planning changed the face of Britain; and the creation of the National Health Service, welfare services and workers' rights greatly improved lives. Factories engaged in war production changed what they had been manufacturing to produce materials to help rebuild Britain, make affordable cars and provide utility clothes and furnishings for its people. A massive programme for the nationalisation of the likes of heavy industry, coal and railways was also instigated, but times would remain austere as the country cleared up its bombed cities and towns and got back on its feet over the next decade. The accepted norms of society had not changed much; many women gave up their wartime jobs as the men returned and once again became housewives running a home and raising a family. There had, however, been enough change to sow the seeds for a different future for their daughters.

FURTHER READING

Briggs, Asa. *Go to It! Working for Victory on the Home Front 1939–1945*. Mitchell Beazley, 2000.

British Rail Press Office. *It Can Now Be Revealed: More About British Railways in Peace and War*. London, 1945.

Bryan, Tim. *Railways in Wartime*. Shire Publications, 2011.

Calder, Angus. *The People's War*. Pimlico, 1969.

Court, W.H.B. *Coal*. HMSO London, 1951.

Davis, Brian L. *British Army Uniforms and Insignia of World War Two*. Arms and Armour Press, 1983.

Gardiner, Juliet. *Wartime Britain 1939–1945*. Headline Review, 2004.

Graves, Charles. *Drive for Freedom*. Hodder & Stoughton, 1945.

Iron and Steel Federation. *The Battle of Steel: A Record of the British Iron and Steel Industry at War*. n.d.

Kay, Fiona and Storey, Neil R. *1940s Fashion*. Amberley, 2018.

Meiggs, Russell. *Home Timber Production 1939–1945*. Crosby Lockwood, 1949.

Nash, George C. *The LMS at War*. London Midland and Scottish Railway, 1946.

Priestley, J.B. *British Women Go to War*. Collins, 1943.

Rodgers, David. *Shadow Factories*. Helion, 2016.

Scott, Peggy. *They Made Invasion Possible*. Hutchinson, 1945.

Storey, Neil R. and Kay, Fiona. *Faces of the Home Front*. Pen and Sword, 2021.

Times, The. *British War Production 1939–1945*. London, 1945.

PLACES TO VISIT

Black Country Living Museum, Tipton Road,
Dudley DY1 4SQ. Telephone: 0121 557 9643
Website: www.bclm.co.uk

Brooklands Museum, Brooklands Road, Weybridge, Surrey
KT13 0SL. Telephone: 01932 857381.
Website: www.brooklandsmuseum.com

Imperial War Museum London, Lambeth Road,
London SE1 6HZ. Telephone: 020 7416 5000.
Website: www.iwm.org.uk

Imperial War Museum North, Trafford Wharf Road, Trafford
Park, Stretford, Manchester M17 1TZ. Telephone: 020
7416 5000. Website: www.iwm.org.uk

Leeds Industrial Museum at Armley Mills, Canal Road,
Armley, Leeds LS12 2QF. Telephone: 0113 378 3173.
Website: museumsandgalleries.leeds.
gov.uk/leeds-industrial-museum

*National Coal Mining Museum for
England*, Caphouse Colliery,
New Rd, Overton, Wakefield
WF4 4RH. Telephone: 01924
848806. Website: www.ncm.org.uk

*Science and Industry
Museum*, Liverpool Road,
Manchester M3 4FP.
Telephone: 0800 047 8124.
Website: www.scienceandindustry
museum.org.uk

The Tank Museum, Linsay Road,
Bovington, Wareham BH20 6JG.
Telephone: 01929 405096.
Website: www.tankmuseum.org

OPPOSITE
One of the
'Caring for
War Workers'
Children is a
National Service'
posters, 1942.

INDEX